Becky
Maicel

© 2003 Harlequin Enterprises Ltd.

Blessings Among the Roses

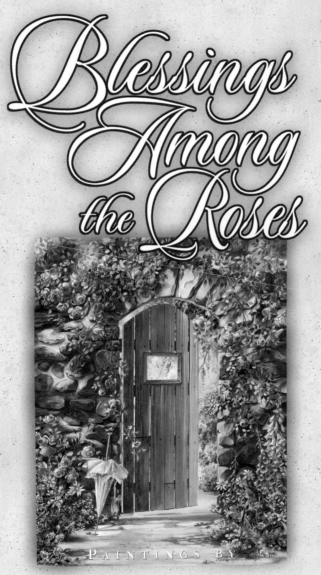

PAINTINGS BY

Sandy Lynam Clough®

HARVEST HOUSE PUBLISHERS
Eugene, Oregon

Blessings Among the Roses

Text Copyright © 2000 Harvest House Publishers
Eugene, Oregon 97402

ISBN 0-7369-0332-1

Sandy Clough Studios
25 Trail Road
Marietta, GA 30064
(800) 447-8409

Design and production by Garborg Design Works, Minneapolis, Minnesota

Harvest House Publishers has made every effort to trace the ownership of all poems and quotes. In the event of a question arising from the use of a poem or quote, we regret any error made and will be pleased to make the necessary correction in future editions of this book.

Printed in Hong Kong

02 03 04 05 06 07 08 09 / NG / 10 9 8 7 6 5 4 3

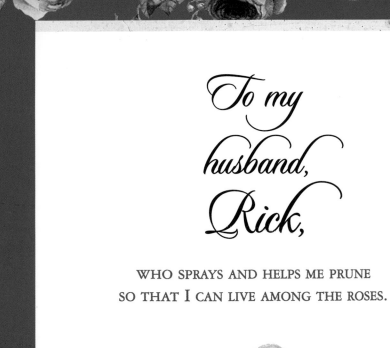

To my husband, Rick,

WHO SPRAYS AND HELPS ME PRUNE
SO THAT I CAN LIVE AMONG THE ROSES.

You can't light a candle to show others the way,
Without feeling the warmth of that bright little ray;
And you can't give a rose all fragrant with dew,
Without some of its sweetness remaining with you.
AUTHOR UNKNOWN

Spring Will Come

We usually do not describe the winter season in our lives in glowing terms. We may think of it as something that will come in our later years. But there may be many "winters" in our lives—times when hope lies dormant and the resources of our hearts seem dried up. These desperate times can come suddenly, too, without the comforting transition of an autumn.

Literally in the midst of a productive summer season, I experienced a threat to my vision. Suddenly and without warning, it was winter in my life. I stepped into a season where I desperately missed the warmth and comfort of the past, regretted the trying circumstances of the present, and feared that the future might be darker and ever colder. In that bleak season, though, I found the secret of new life and growth. No, my friend, winter is not the end. It is a new beginning.

For in that hostile climate of disappointing circumstances, the roots of my heart began digging deeper than ever. I was searching for the security of an anchor and a source of nourishment—if not enough to grow, at least enough to survive. My roots reached into God's Word as my heart reached out for His Heart. As I was fed by the Psalms in His Word, I waited and waited and waited. After many weeks had passed, I began to notice that winter had a special peace and even a rest about it as God Himself brought a serenity and encouragement to me that I could not provide for myself. With this peace came an amazing contentment and the realization that, if necessary, I could live in this winter day by day.

As my roots tapped into Life Himself, hope began to course through the branches of my heart. Joy began to push out buds of new life. Spring had come! A new confidence in the love and goodness of God enveloped me with the fragrance of faith, hope, and love in the same way that branches laden with roses embrace us with the beauty of spring.

If you find yourself in a winter so deep you cannot forecast spring, do not waste your winter. Let your roots reach and

stretch deeply for real life in God's Word. It is there that He reveals His very heart to us! It's only a matter of time before the roses will follow with their fragrance of faith, hope, and love just for you!

Even with good vision in only one eye, my winter is over. I am experiencing the springtime of God's love and goodness, and it is the most inviting and promising spring I have ever known. I wanted to paint spring for you and invite you, too, to live among the roses.

Sandy

The Fragrance of Faith

FAITH RESTS NOT IN OURSELVES BUT IN THE LORD,
WHOSE VERY LIFE HAS THE POWER OF NEW BIRTH
AND NEW LIFE.

Now faith is being sure of what we hope
for and certain of what we do not see.

THE BOOK OF HEBREWS

Faith is love taking the form of aspiration.

WILLIAM ELLERY CHANNIN

Faith is like a radar that sees through the fog—the reality of things at a distance that the human eye cannot see.
CORRIE TEN BOOM

The smallest seed of faith is better than
the largest fruit of happiness.
HENRY DAVID THOREAU

Faith is to believe what you do not see; the reward of this faith is to see what you believe.
SAINT AUGUSTINE

The principal part of faith is patience.
GEORGE MACDONALD

Every tomorrow has two handles. We can take hold
of it with the handle of anxiety or the handle of faith.

HENRY WARD BEECHER

*Patience with others is Love, Patience with
self is Hope, Patience with God is Faith.*

ADEL BESTAVROS

Faith is the first factor in a life devoted to service. Without it,
nothing is possible. With it, nothing is impossible.
MARY MCLEOD BETHUNE

The beginning of faith is the beginning of fruitfulness...
JOHANN WOLFGANG VON GOETHE

What a wonderful thing it is to be sure of one's faith!
GEORGE FREDERICK HANDEL

We walk by faith, not by sight.
THE BOOK OF 2 CORINTHIANS

*A little faith will bring your soul
to heaven, but a lot of faith will
bring heaven to your soul.*

DWIGHT LYMAN MOODY

Faith is not belief without proof, but
trust without reservation.

D. ELTON TRUEBLOOD

Faith, like sight, is nothing apart
from God. You might as well shut
your eyes and look inside, and see
whether you have sight as to look
inside to discover whether you have faith.

HANNAH WHITALL SMITH

Understanding is the reward of faith.

SAINT AUGUSTINE

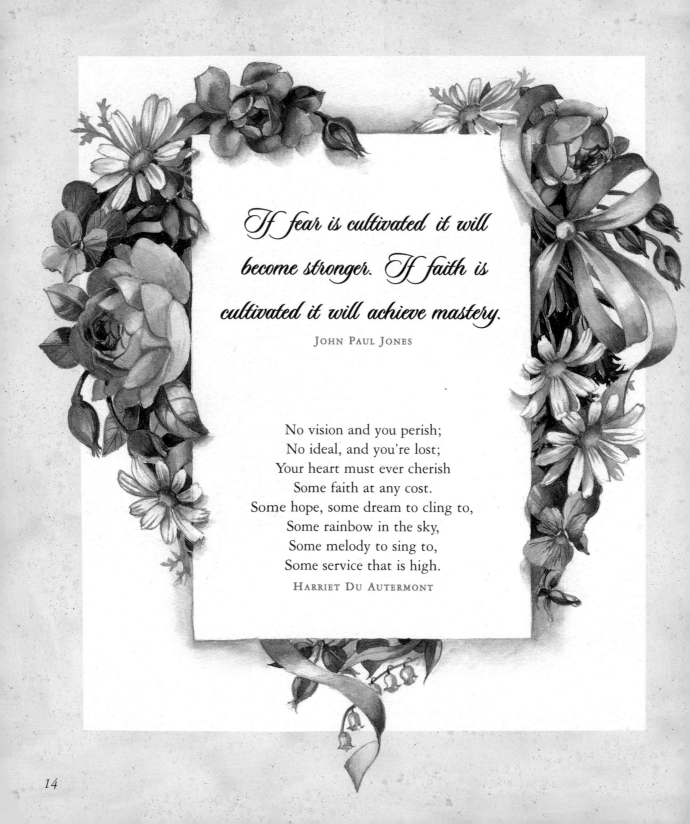

If fear is cultivated it will become stronger. If faith is cultivated it will achieve mastery.

JOHN PAUL JONES

No vision and you perish;
No ideal, and you're lost;
Your heart must ever cherish
Some faith at any cost.
Some hope, some dream to cling to,
Some rainbow in the sky,
Some melody to sing to,
Some service that is high.

HARRIET DU AUTERMONT

Faith has to do with things that are not seen,
and hope with things that are not in hand.
SAINT THOMAS AQUINAS

The only thing that counts is faith

expressing itself through love.

THE BOOK OF GALATIANS

Faith is deliberate confidence in the character of
God whose ways you may not understand at the time.
OSWALD CHAMBERS

I see heaven's glories shine and faith shines equal...

EMILY BRONTË

Faith is like electricity. You can't see it, but you can see the light.
SOURCE UNKNOWN

Sandy Lynam Clough

If we were logical, the future would

be bleak indeed. But we are more than logical. We are

human beings, and we have faith, and we have hope...

JACQUES COUSTEAU

Faith is the virtue of the storm,

just as happiness is the virtue of sunshine.

RUTH BENEDICT

We give thanks to God always for you all, making mention of
you in our prayers; remembering without ceasing your work of faith, and
labor of love, and patience of hope in our Lord Jesus Christ....
THE BOOK OF 1 THESSALONIANS

Sandy Lynam Clough

Faith, mighty faith the promise sees

And rests on that alone:

Laughs at impossibilities,

And says it shall be done.

CHARLES WESLEY

Sandy Lynam Clough

The Fragrance of Hope

HOPE IS THE CONFIDENCE THAT EVEN THOUGH MORE WIN-
TERS WILL SURELY COME, EVEN MORE CERTAINLY THE ROSES
WILL FOLLOW IN AN EVER-INCREASING ABUNDANCE.

The eyes of the LORD are on those…
whose hope is in his unfailing love.
THE BOOK OF PSALMS

Hope is a waking dream.

ARISTOTLE

Hope is a strange invention—
A Patent of the Heart—
In unremitting action
Yet never wearing out.

EMILY DICKINSON

Ah, Hope! What would life be, stripped of thy
encouraging smiles, that teach us to look behind
the dark clouds of today, for the golden beams
that are to gild the morrow.
SUSANNA MOODIE

Hope is the thing with feathers
That perches in the soul,
And sings the tune without words
And never stops, at all.
EMILY DICKINSON

The hope of the righteous shall be gladness...

THE BOOK OF PROVERBS

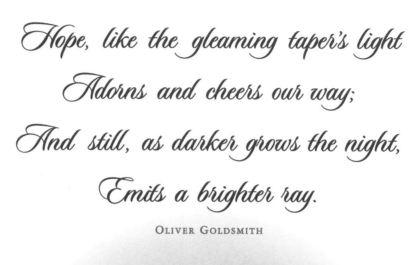

Hope, like the gleaming taper's light

Adorns and cheers our way;

And still, as darker grows the night,

Emits a brighter ray.

OLIVER GOLDSMITH

Sandy Lynam Clough

May the God of hope fill you with all
joy and peace as you trust in him, so
that you may overflow with hope…

THE BOOK OF ROMANS

Hope springs eternal...

ALEXANDER POPE

He who has hope has everything.

ARABIAN PROVERB

No winter lasts forever; no spring skips its turn.

HAL BORLAND

Words can be
beautiful.
So can dreams.
So can hopes.

F. CLIFTON WHITE

Hope is

outreaching desire

with expectancy

of good.

EDWARD S. AMES

There is no medicine like hope, no incentive so great, and no tonic so powerful as expectation of something tomorrow.

ORISON SWETT MARDEN

Hope is faith in the future tense.

PETER ANDERSON

Nothing that is worth anything can be achieved in a lifetime; therefore we must be saved by hope.

REINHOLD NIEBUHR

What a strange thing is memory, and hope; one looks backward, the other forward; one is of today, the other of tomorrow.

GRANDMA MOSES

Please come for tea ~ Sandy

Sandy Lyman Clough

Hope can see heaven
through the thickest clouds.
THOMAS BROOKS

O Hope! dazzling, radiant Hope!—

What a change thou bringest to the

hopeless; brightening the darkened paths,

and cheering the lonely way.

AIMEE SEMPLE MCPHERSON

Honor begets honor; trust begets
trust; faith begets faith; and hope is
the mainspring of life.
HENRY LEWIS STIMSON

Without God there is for mankind no purpose, no goal, no hope, only a wavering future...

JEAN PAUL

Of all the forces that make for a better world,
none is so indispensable, none so powerful,
as hope. Without hope men are only half alive.
With hope they think and dream and work.

CHARLES SAWYER

Hope is never ill when faith is well.

JOHN BUNYAN

Sandy Lynam Clough

The Fragrance of Love

KNOWING AND EXPERIENCING BEING LOVED JUST AS I AM
IMPARTS A JOY THAT JUST HAS TO BE SHARED.

Love and faithfulness meet together...

THE BOOK OF PSALMS

Without His love I can do nothing,
with His love there is nothing I cannot do.
AUTHOR UNKNOWN

Love is a fruit in season at all times,
and within the reach of every hand.
MOTHER TERESA

Love changes darkness into light and

makes the heart take a "wingless flight."

HELEN STEINER RICE

Our doubts do not destroy God's love,
nor does our faith create it. It originates in
the very nature of God, who is love...
JERRY BRIDGES

Consider the great love of the Lord.

THE BOOK OF PSALMS

The highest love
of all finds its
fulfillment not in
what it keeps, but in
what it gives.

FATHER ANDREW

Sandy Lynam Clough

Dear friends, let us love one another, for love comes from God.

THE BOOK OF 1 JOHN

May no gift be too small to give, nor too simple to receive, which is wrapped in thoughtfulness, and tied with love.

L.O. BAIRD

Love is a great beautifier.

LOUISA MAY ALCOTT

Because of the Lord's great love, we are not consumed, for his compassions never fail.

THE BOOK OF LAMENTATIONS

Everyone has inside
of him a piece of good news. The good news
is that you don't know how great you can be!
How much you can love!

ANNE FRANK

Many waters cannot quench

love, neither can floods drown it.

THE SONG OF SOLOMON

Love is a force more formidable than any other. It is invisible—it
cannot be seen or measured, yet it is powerful enough to transform you in
a moment, and offer you more joy than any material possession could.

BARBARA DE ANGELIS

The love we give away is

the only love we keep.

ELBERT HUBBARD

Love

Sandy Lynam Clough

*God loves each of us
as if there were only one of us.*

SAINT AUGUSTINE

When you know how much God is in love with you
then you can only live your life radiating that love.
MOTHER TERESA

God is love;

His mercy brightens

All the path in which we rove;

Bliss He wakes

And woe He lightens;

God is wisdom,

God is love.

JOHN BOWRING

Let us but feel that He has His heart set upon us, that
He is watching us from those heavens with tender interest,
that He is following us day by day as a mother follows her
babe in his first attempt to walk alone, that He has set
His love upon us, and in spite of ourselves is working
out for us His highest will and blessing...

A.B. SIMPSON

Of all the earthly music, that which reaches
farthest into heaven is the beating of a truly loving heart.

HENRY WARD BEECHER

No one has ever seen God;

but if we love each other,

God lives in us and

his love is made complete in us.

THE BOOK OF 1 JOHN

You can give
without loving,
but you cannot love
without giving.

AMY CARMICHAEL

Sandy Lynam Clough

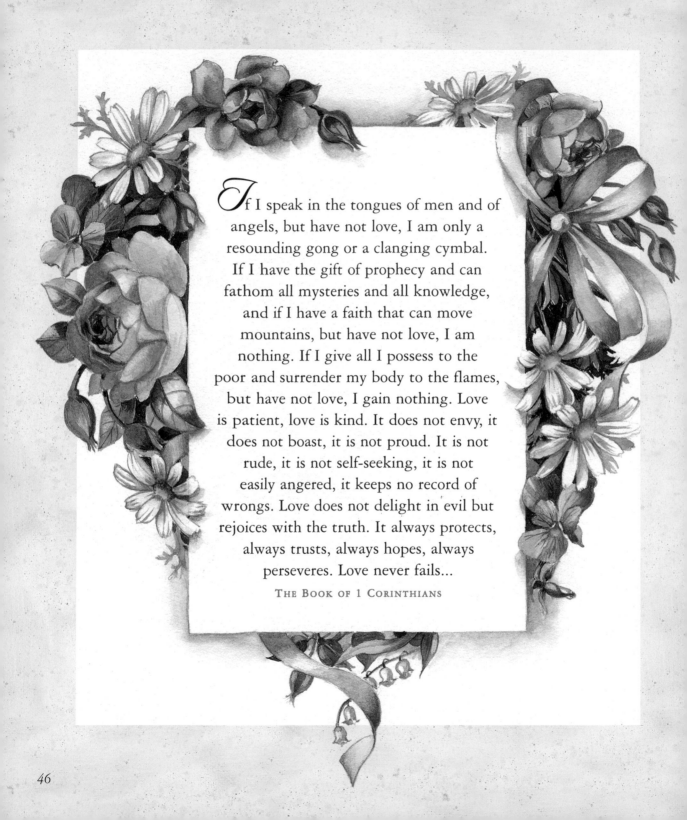

If I speak in the tongues of men and of angels, but have not love, I am only a resounding gong or a clanging cymbal. If I have the gift of prophecy and can fathom all mysteries and all knowledge, and if I have a faith that can move mountains, but have not love, I am nothing. If I give all I possess to the poor and surrender my body to the flames, but have not love, I gain nothing. Love is patient, love is kind. It does not envy, it does not boast, it is not proud. It is not rude, it is not self-seeking, it is not easily angered, it keeps no record of wrongs. Love does not delight in evil but rejoices with the truth. It always protects, always trusts, always hopes, always perseveres. Love never fails...

THE BOOK OF 1 CORINTHIANS

Joy is a light that fills you with hope and faith and love.

And now these three remain: faith, hope and love. But the greatest of these is love.

THE BOOK OF 1 CORINTHIANS

48